IN THE WINGS

21ST CENTURY PLAYS

IN THE WINGS

a new comedy by
Stewart F. Lane

PERFORMING BOOKS

A PERFORMING BOOKS ORIGINAL

For all prospective productions, professional and amateur, kindly apply to Stellar Productions, 36 West 44th Street, Suite 400, New York, NY 10036, phone 212-315-0402, fax 212-307-5489, www.mrbroadway.com.

Substantial discounts are available on multiple-copy purchases of this play for rehearsal and production purposes.

Publisher's Cataloging-in-Publication

Lane, Stewart F.
   In the wings : a new comedy / by Stewart F. Lane.—1st ed.—New York, NY : Performing Books, c2008
      p. ; cm.
      (21st century plays)
      ISBN: 978-1-55783-738-7
      1. Theater—Drama. 2. Actors—Drama. 3. Actresses—Drama.
    4. Theater—New York (State)—New York—Drama. I. Title.

PS3612.A549 I58 2008
812.6—dc22   0805

ACKNOWLEDGMENTS

I would like to thank my wonderful wife,
Bonnie, for her continued suport and encouragement.

IN THE WINGS…was presented as a reading by Stellar Productions, Intl. Inc. at the Revelation Theater in New York City on May 25, 2004. It was directed by Tony-Award-winning producer Stewart F. Lane. The cast was as follows:

CAST

Melinda Donahugh	Shannen Doherty
Nicky Sanchez	Luke McFarlane
Steve Leonards	John Krasinski
Bernardo	Olek Krupa
Martha Leonards	Jana Robbins
Stage Directions	Madeleine Maby

Casting by	Liz Lewis & Elizabeth Bunnell
General Management	Gindi Theatrical Management

IN THE WINGS...had its world premiere off-Broadway at the Promenade Theatre in New York City on September 28, 2005. It was produced by Bonnie Comley & Stellar Productions, Intl. Inc. It was directed by Jeremy Dobrish. The cast was as follows:

CAST

Melinda Donahugh	Lisa Datz
Nicky Sanchez	Brian Henderson
Steve Leonards	Josh Prince
Bernardo	Peter Scolari
Martha Leonards	Marilyn Sokol

Sets	William Barclay
Costumes	Mattie Ullrich
Lighting	Phil Monat
Sound Designer	Jill B C DuBoff
Production Stage Manager	Pamela Edington
General Production Manager	Roger Alan Gindi

UNDERSTUDIES

Understudies never substitute for listed performers unless a specific announcement is made at the time of the performance.

Melinda	Carrie Keranen
Nicky	John Coppola
Steve	Brian Henderson
Bernardo	Mitchell Greenberg
Martha	Maria Cellario

IN THE WINGS

IN THE WINGS

Time & Place
New York City, 1977

CHARACTERS

Steve Leonards . . . . Late twenties,
enthusiastic actor

Melinda Donahugh . . . . Late twenties,
enthusiastic actress,
Steve's live-in girlfriend

Nicky Sanchez. . . . . Mid-thirties, street smart

Bernardo . . . . Early fifties, respected
acting teacher, director,
playwright, you name it

Martha Leonards . . . . Early sixties, Steve's mother,
from New Jersey

ACT I SCENE I

It is late afternoon in mid-September. The curtain rises on the one-bedroom apartment shared by Steve Leonards and Melinda Donahugh. It looks like the abode of two struggling actors. Eclectic furniture, a sofa, big easy chair, coffee table, two barrels holding up a door for a table. There is a telephone down center and some bottles of booze on a table by the kitchen.

Melinda is sitting on the sofa with a drink in one hand and a cigarette in the other. Nicky enters and quickly locks the door behind him. After making sure he wasn't followed, he makes a drink and downs it. He drinks it as if it were water. He gives a weary look to Melinda, makes another drink and finishes that one. He starts to make another, when Melinda puts her arms around him.

MELINDA. You've been through an enormous pseudo Slavic day in court, my poor dear. My poor, poor crazy Czar of my heart. When you face the committee tomorrow, I know you will do the perspicacious thing. Tomorrow, the world will comprehend the meaning of the word "harlot."

NICKY. Harlot?

MELINDA. Hero, I mean hero. You're so detached, yet so together. So wired, yet so loose.

Nicky raises his hand.

NICKY. When I…

MELINDA. No, don't speak. Save your enormous tongue and your enormous lips for that enormous microphone tomorrow. I will do all the speaking. And when I speak, other people will talk, and when they do, it won't be about the Hollywood Ten. It will be about the Hollywood Eleven. If there is anything I can give you or, maybe, do for you…I have such an overpowering urge to make a personal sacrifice for the revolution.

They kiss and fall onto the sofa. Steve Leonards enters with several record albums and groceries in hand. He doesn't see them behind the sofa, but he sees the bottle of vodka and proceeds to make himself a drink. Taking a sip, he realizes it's water and spits it out.

STEVE. Bogus booze!

MELINDA. Oh!

STEVE. When vodka tastes like water, it's time to get on the wagon.

NICKY. It *is* water.

MELINDA. Hi, honey.

STEVE. Hi, hot stuff. Hey, who's the real boyfriend here?

He kisses Melinda.

NICKY. Get a room.

STEVE. This is our room.

NICKY. You guys are gross. I'm going home. I gotta use the bathroom.

He exits to the bathroom.

STEVE. What are you guys rehearsing?

MELINDA. We're still rehearsing Gladys's big scene at the end of Act 1.

STEVE. How's it going?

MELINDA. I've had to kiss Nicky all afternoon—how do you think its going? Oh Steve, I wish I was doing the scene with you. I've missed you today.

They kiss.

STEVE. So what's Bernardo's new play called this week?

MELINDA. *I Married a Communist.*

Nicky enters from the bathroom.

NICKY. It's not exactly a new play. Bernardo's been working on it for what? Twenty years?

STEVE. Since the day his father died.

MELINDA. He relives the anguish, degradation and humiliation he felt when his father went before the House Un-American Activities Committee.

STEVE. Good things take time. Like fine wine and actors. Do you want to be the Three Stooges or Robert Redford?

NICKY. What's wrong with the Three Stooges? Curly was really very funny. They were unique in the annals of comedy. What with their split-second timing and those amazing sound effects.

Nicky starts to make noises and movements like the Three Stooges. Steve and Melinda stare. He stops.

MELINDA. Anyway, if we have to, we'll have time before class.

NICKY. For what? I forgot what we were talking about.

MELINDA. Our scene?

NICKY. I know the key to the character is in those lines.

MELINDA. You don't have any lines.

NICKY. Their feelings for each other are growing, swelling, straining, soon to burst and pour forth with a too-nami of lust and passion. I'm going to work on it at home.

STEVE. Just don't stain the sheets. Hey honey, where's the real stuff?

Pouring the water in his glass into a plant.

MELINDA. I poured it into a carton of orange juice.

STEVE. The breakfast of champions. There's water in the vodka, iced tea in the scotch bottle, and vodka in the O.J.

NICKY. So Steverino, Mel said you were out making the rounds today.

MELINDA. Any luck, my love?

STEVE. I found ten different ways to say, "Hi, I'm a doormat."

NICKY. I've held a lot of different jobs in my time. Construction worker, pool boy, private detective, male escort....

STEVE. Private dick and public dick.

NICKY. Yeah, Pinkerton. West coast. Anyway, like I was saying, I've paid my dues to a lot of clubs, but acting has got to be the hardest gig of all.

MELINDA. You haven't got an acting gig yet.

NICKY. I make a point of getting my name in front of the agents every week.

STEVE. Don't they get sick of you?

NICKY. Naw. I make up as a different actor each time. I have four different eight by ten glossies. I have four different resumes and I go to four different psychiatrists to keep them all straight...or gay as the case may be.

STEVE. What's happening with *I Married A Communist*? Is Bernardo doing the showcase or what?

NICKY. One week he's into it—we're on—next week he's not sure if the public is ready.

MELINDA. That's the price you pay for being a genius.

NICKY. I should get paid for my geniusness. What is he waiting for? Everyone knows I'd be perfect for the part of the lawyer, Roy Cohn.

STEVE. You may be perfectly adequate, but I am ideal. It just so happens, I have been brushing up on my jurisprudence.

Steve takes out a book.

NICKY. Listen up, Prudence. That part is off the court docket as far as you're concerned.

STEVE. Oh, yeah, who died and made you judge?

NICKY. That part is mine.

STEVE. In your dreams.

NICKY. You bet in my dreams. And I dream big, my friend, real big. Adios, losers.

Nicky exits.

MELINDA. So was it a disaster today?

STEVE. It's funny how tired a man can get after making the rounds…

MELINDA. You poor comrade, sit down.

STEVE. I must have walked the whole length of Broadway. If someone massaged my feet, my mind could concentrate on the more important events of the day.

MELINDA. Allow me.

> *She begins to massage his feet.*

STEVE. Ah, that's better. I was walking by Bernardo's studio.

MELINDA. He was there?

STEVE. He wasn't there.

MELINDA. I'm warning you.

STEVE. A little more into the arch.

MELINDA. This better be good.

STEVE. Oh, it's very good.

MELINDA. Concentrate.

STEVE. No, he wasn't there. But a certain tight-assed assistant was.

MELINDA. Cleo? What did he say?

STEVE. Don't stop, please, don't stop.

Melinda squeezes his foot.

Owwwww! Hey! Okay, okay. The play, she is ready. Cleo said Bernardo was looking for us, and wanted us at home to take his call between seven and eight.

MELINDA. Bernardo, Calling here? Oh Steve, you'd be a brilliant Roy Cohn. I would be perfect for the role Gladys, the saucy sister from Vladivostok.

STEVE. My mother always wanted me to be a lawyer.

MELINDA. Your mother wanted you to be anything but an actor. Do you realize we've been studying with Bernardo for three years now?

STEVE. Do I realize? I've paid him nineteen thousand two hundred and forty-two dollars in tuition as of last night's class—that I missed.

MELINDA. Oh, Steve, baby, this could be the break. God, I've gotten nothing up until now. I figured a soap opera, a commercial, something.

STEVE. You had that great job in the food commercial.

MELINDA. I was the fortieth raisin in a bowl of cereal. I stood in milk for three hours.

STEVE. You had very creamy skin.

Cuddling up to her.

MELINDA. At least you've got credits and you've got a job. You're working on the radio station…on the air!

STEVE. "Hello listeners, yes, it's Christmas once again. And, as always, as regular as clock work, it's time for Tchaikovsky's *Nutcracker Suite* as orchestrated by Bruce Springsteen and performed by the Chipmunks."

MELINDA. You're in show business. Speaking of the station, Pete called. He really wants you there full time.

STEVE. It's a full-time graveyard, Mel.

MELINDA. I only bring it up because your mother called today. I'm sorry. I told her about the job at the station.

STEVE. Et tu, Mel? How could you?

MELINDA. I panicked, she was going on and on…and I didn't know what to say. I figured she'd be proud.

STEVE. Do you realize how long I'm going to hear about this?

Imitating his mother.

So, boychick? Why don't you take the job at the station? If you'd taken the job at the station, like I told you, you'd have a steady paycheck today.

MELINDA. I said I was sorry. It's just so hard asking my parents for money all the time. They just don't have it and I have a brother struggling in the film industry.

Pause.

Oh, Jesus, what time is it?

STEVE. Seven fifteen.

MELINDA. He's not calling. You heard wrong. You only heard what you wanted to hear and he's not going to call.

STEVE. Look, we're driving each other crazy with this. Let's take inventory. You first. Be positive.

MELINDA. I lost five pounds.

STEVE. Model thin.

MELINDA. My face is good, clear…my body's tight.

STEVE. Like a drum.

MELINDA. My breasts are high and firm.

STEVE. Stratospheric and extremely firm.

MELINDA. Everything I eat goes straight to my ass.

STEVE. It's a pretty…

He goes to pinch her. The phone rings.

STEVE & MELINDA. It's him!

Steve and Mel run for the phone. Mel answers.

MELINDA. Hello Bernardo?

Listens.

Oh, hi! Steve, it's my mother.

Steve exits to bedroom.

Hello mother, dahling. Greetings from New York City, the entertainment capital of the world. I haven't got much time. I'm expecting a very important call any minute now, so I have to talk fast. I might have a role in an important new play. This is everything you ever dreamed of for me. It could lead to TV. And movies—oh Momma, big box office blockbusters. And mother, you and papa wouldn't have to send checks to me anymore. I'd send checks to you. Big fat checks. Both of you could retire and I could take care of you for a change. Wouldn't that be nice? All I need is a little extra cash and a little more time. It's the last time I'll ask for it. I mean it. Last time, I swear. I mean it. Okay. No, of course I understand, really. Love you too. Good-bye.

STEVE. What's the matter?

MELINDA. She's a doll, but she has this warped concept about me and the business. She thinks it's all about TV appearances and performing with movie stars. She doesn't get it that the joy is in the work, the craft.

STEVE. What if she is right and we're wrong?

MELINDA. If I couldn't pay my share of the rent, I'd have to go back…there! You have to mortgage your mother to live in this town.

STEVE. You could mortgage mine.

MELINDA. Unless, maybe, if you worked full time at the station…

STEVE. Mel.

MELINDA. Full-time for just a little while.

STEVE. I'm trying to start a career too, you know?

MELINDA. I know. It's just that I'm near the end of my rope and I'm desperate.

STEVE. I tell you what I'm willing to do. If I don't get the show, I'll consider it. I'll leave the door open on that, okay?

MELINDA. Oh, Steve, you're the greatest.

The buzzer rings from downstairs.

STEVE & MELINDA. It's him!

Melinda and Steve go for the phone. Melinda answers again.

MELINDA. Hello? Bernardo? He's not there.

The buzzer rings again. Steve goes to the intercom.

STEVE. Hello?

BERNARDO. Hello? Hello, lambs. It's your guru and savior. I was in the neighborhood and I thought I'd stop by for a chat.

STEVE. Sure, take your time. It's the fifth floor.

MELINDA. Do you want us to come down to you?

BERNARDO. Don't be silly. I'm not an old man.

> *Steve goes to the door. They both stare down the staircase, waiting for Bernardo. He appears huffing and puffing, trying to catch his breath.*

STEVE. Are you all right?

> *Bernardo nods yes.*

Would you like a glass of water?

> *He shakes no.*

MELINDA. Would you like a glass of wine?

> *He shakes no. He takes out a handkerchief and wipes his brow.*

STEVE. How about vodka?

Bernardo nods yes. Melinda shakes her head no showing the empty bottle of vodka.

What about a screwdriver?

Still catching his breath, Bernardo nods vigorously. Melinda grabs a glass and ice and gets the orange juice carton and starts to pour it in front of him.

BERNARDO. That's quite a health club you have in this building. Nostrovya.

Bernardo downs it in one draught.

Thank you, lamb.

MELINDA. Come sit down.

BERNARDO. I don't usually make house calls. Now I remember why. Oh, whew, yes, now that's better. How are my flocks today?

MELINDA. We're fine.

BERNARDO. Gather 'round, children. Take hold of your senses. Now wait. You both look so tense, so pale, so on edge.

MELINDA. We're fine, really.

BERNARDO. Not another word until we have done "Bernardo's Relaxation Exercise, number five."

They go through a ritual where Steve and Mel act as if in a trance like state.

Breath in, breath out. Mo-Mo-Mo-Mo. Relax, Maa Maa. Repeat after me. Ommmmmmmm. Ommmmmmmm. Obee, obee…wan wan…kenobi, kenobi, kenobi. I am at peace.

STEVE & MELINDA. I am at peace.

BERNARDO. I am at rest.

STEVE & MELINDA. I am at rest.

BERNARDO. I am at one with Bernardo.

STEVE & MELINDA. I am at one with Bernardo.

BERNARDO. Breath and done. I feel much better how about you?

STEVE & MELINDA. Great! Wow. Much better. Yeah, very loose.

BERNARDO. I can only stay a few minutes, anyway. I'm on my way to a production meeting.

STEVE. For *I Married A Communist*?

BERNARDO. No, *My Fair Lady*! Of course for *I Married a Communist*. Finally, after all this time, my play is ready to be produced. As you know, my play, my baby, was twenty years in the making—talk about your labor pains—but now, it is ready to make its appearance. The title has changed over the years: *I Was Engaged to the Communist Party, Run Red, Run Scared, A Communist Married Me*, and finally, my favorite, *The Red Party Rag*. But the producers, tasteless money men, thought it sounded too upbeat. So, *I Married a Communist* was born. The titles may change, but the thrust of the piece remained eternal.

STEVE. Which is?

BERNARDO. The mystery of life, my dear boy. Being thrust into an untenable situation. Democracy being shaken to its very core. It was a dark and terrible time for all those who sacrificed for the cause. Blacklisted, hungry, jobless, homeless…

STEVE. You were homeless?

BERNARDO. Nyet, comrade. My father. They called him a Red, a pinko. But for all that pain and agony they left him off the list.

MELINDA. The Hollywood Ten.

BERNARDO. Da, exactly. It should have been the Hollywood Eleven. As a result, history has forgotten papa…until now. Until opening night when a chorus of actors will cry his story to the catwalks and make history…

MELINDA. I was just rehearsing that last scene in the first act in which Gladys opens herself up, body and soul, to the revolutionary fervor. That there's not anything she would not do for the cause.

BERNARDO. Oh, yes, I love that scene. It's in all the versions. That scene worked from the very beginning. Yes, a very strong scene…worked the first time, every time. I've been giving that scene to my students for years. Gave me time to really get to know my students…and work on the scene, of course. Et voilà!

He takes out a script from his bag.

MELINDA. That's it?

BERNARDO. Mais, oui.

STEVE. Why are you speaking French?

BERNARDO. My dear boy, English is for the stage and everyday life. Russian is for politics. But when I am truly happy, only French will do, n'est-ce pas? By the way, very socialist, the French, you know.

Melinda grabs the script.

MELINDA. Is this for me? I never in a million years...oh, Bernardo! There are so many talented people for you to choose from.

BERNARDO. You think I'm being too hasty?

MELINDA. I'm better than all of them.

STEVE. That was really great of you to come by and give it to Mel, personally and all.

BERNARDO. You're jumping ahead, my boy. Always remember to stay in the moment. This one's for you.

He hands another script to Steve.

I want you to play Roy Cohn, the lawyer.

STEVE. No objection here, your honor.

BERNARDO. Nice start. You're a little young, but with a few modest suggestions from the right director, you might win a Tony.

To Melinda.

You, my pet, are another thing altogether.

MELINDA. Uh-oh.

BERNARDO. The competition was fierce. But the muses were on your side. Melinda, I would like to offer you the lead role of beautiful, lusty, sexy, sensuous, Gladys the nun.

MELINDA. Oh, yes, yes. Thank you, thank you. I'm overwhelmed.

BERNARDO. Mais oui, but of course you are. We'll all have plenty of time to show each other our appreciation in the next few weeks. Three weeks rehearsal, including some class time, and we run for sixteen performances. No pay, of course, my pets—it is a showcase. But think of the exposure of being in my play! I don't have to tell you that every major critic in town will show up. Well, I must go and attend to others in my flock.

MELINDA. Is Nicky in it?

BERNARDO. Quel dommage. No, sorry, a little rough around the edges…too Sylvester Stallone-ish, if you know what I mean.

STEVE. Nicky's Protestant from the Pacific Northwest.

BERNARDO. Too Paul Bunyon-esque. You get my drift? In the words of the great Noel Coward, "Don't quibble, Syble." Dostvadonya, Rehearsals start Monday. Bonsoir and bonne chance.

In the doorway, looking at the stairs.

At least it's all downhill from here.

END OF ACT I SCENE I.

ACT I SCENE II

Melinda is seen in a spotlight in front of the mirror in the bedroom. She is holding a hairbrush like it was a trophy.

MELINDA. Of course, I would like to thank the League and the American Theater Wing for this honor. It is both a humbling and exhilarating experience at the same time. I would most like to thank my mentor, Miss Margo Channing, without whose help I could never have beat out Eve Harrington for this award… and of course, my mother and father. Mother! Oh, shit, I forgot to call Mom. Ladies and gentlemen, I am so sorry I have to win the award and run, but I forgot to call my mother with the good news about getting the role in the play…that you just gave me the award for in the first place. Family, you know. Thank you, thank you.

> *She blows a kiss to the mirror and lights out.*

> *END OF ACT I SCENE II*

ACT I SCENE III

Same day, afternoon. Steve enters in his jogging clothes and makes a beeline for the bathroom. The light goes on and we hear a tinkle.

STEVE. Ow, wow.

> *The toilet flushes. We hear him turn the water on in the shower. He sings.*

I'm the top, I'm the Coliseum, I'm the top, I'm the Louvre Museum, I'm a melody from a symphony by Strauss…

> *There is a knock at the door. After a moment Martha enters, with her own key, catching her breath, and carrying a bag of groceries.*

MARTHA. Hello? My God, who needs to join a gym after that? Those stairs alone will kill you. Hello?

> *No one answers. She notices a pair of panty hose on the sofa. Shaking her head, she goes to the kitchen to unpack the bag. She starts to make some instant coffee.*

My son, the Jewish Bob Goulet. Honey, it's Mother. Do you want some coffee?

Steve doesn't answer. She walks over to the bathroom door.

Do you want some coffee?

STEVE. Sure. Great.

She goes back to the kitchen.

You're early. Is everything all right?

He turns the shower off and enters wrapped in a towel.

I have a surprise for you, Mel.

He's about to flash her when he sees his mother enter with a plate of cookies.

Mom!

MARTHA. Is that how you greet your mother?

STEVE. What the hell are you doing here?

Steve realizes he's wearing a towel, so he grabs an aviator jacket from the closet. It covers him from the waist up.

MARTHA. Oh, that's much better.

He takes off the jacket and exchanges it for a raincoat.

STEVE. If this towel falls off. I'll be in therapy for a decade.

MARTHA. Honey, I was at your bris.

STEVE. Would you cut that out?

MARTHA. Career change?

STEVE. How did you get in here? Where's Mel? What did you do with Mel?

MARTHA. I've kidnapped her. She's in a locker in Larchmont. You won't see her until Tisha-b'Av unless you call more often. I haven't heard from you in weeks. I come bearing Mallomars and all I get is the third degree.

STEVE. Sorry, Mom.

He kisses her.

I thought you were Mel.

MARTHA. If that's how you greet her, it's no wonder she likes living with you.

STEVE. That's just the tip of the iceberg.

MARTHA. Like father, like son.

She hands him the panty hose.

Here. Are these yours?

STEVE. Yes and you can't have them.

MARTHA. Well, you never know.

STEVE. Wait—what if they *were* mine?

MARTHA. Well then, I'd buy you a nice pair of pumps to match.

STEVE. How did you get in here?

MARTHA. The door was open.

STEVE. It was?

MARTHA. You should be more careful. Remember, you're not in Scarsdale anymore. I could have been a burglar.

STEVE. Burglars I can handle. You, I like to be prepared for.

MARTHA. I'll take that as a compliment.

STEVE. Why is it that whenever I try to take a shower you seem to call or show up on my doorstep?

MARTHA. Call it a mother's gift. Timing is everything. Are you dressing properly? It's getting cold outside.

STEVE. Yeah, I bundle up warm these days. Mel takes good care of me.

MARTHA. She's out? Your goy toy?

STEVE. Very funny, Mother. She's out. She's at class.

MARTHA. Still studying with that Svengali? Leonardo? That shyster, that gonif who takes your money…

STEVE. Bernardo, Mom. His name is Bernardo, and he's no shyster. He's one of the most respected teachers in the business. The biggest movie stars in the world go to him just to learn how to act.

MARTHA. Stars need to learn how to act?

STEVE. Sure. Just because they're stars doesn't mean they can act.

MARTHA. Oh.

STEVE. The fact is, most of the time they don't know how to act—they just know how to make big money.

MARTHA. Can Bernardo teach you how to make big money?

STEVE. Not exactly.

MARTHA. Then what good is he? Why don't the stars teach you?

STEVE. Because stars don't teach acting classes, and they don't teach people how to make big money.

MARTHA. Why not? It would make perfect sense.

STEVE. Because they're not bankers—they're stars and they're too busy…

MARTHA. …making big money. So who needs to teach?

STEVE. Let's just skip it, okay? The point is Bernardo says I'm getting better all the time. He says I just haven't experienced real pain yet.

MARTHA. You want pain? You can have the pain in my heart. Does he at least guarantee you a job?

STEVE. No, he doesn't guarantee me a job. But it just so happens Bernardo is directing his new play and he wants me and Mel to be in it.

MARTHA. What's it called?

STEVE. *I Married a Communist.*

MARTHA. How charming. I didn't know you and Melinda were so politically inclined. Or are you trying to tell me something else? Oh my God. You got married and Melinda's a Communist!

STEVE. No, I didn't get married.

MARTHA. You're sure.

STEVE. Pretty sure.

MARTHA. And Melinda's not a card-carrying Communist?

STEVE. No, she's a credit-card–carrying consumer capitalist.

MARTHA. God bless her.

STEVE. *I Married a Communist* is simply the name of the show. There's no hidden agenda.

MARTHA. I never heard of it.

STEVE. Well, of course you never heard of it. It's never been done before.

MARTHA. A Broadway show?

STEVE. No, it's a showcase.

MARTHA. How much do they pay you?

STEVE. No pay.

MARTHA. What mother wouldn't be proud? Will anyone come see you? Besides your father and me, I mean.

STEVE. Agents may come, critics, maybe some casting directors, but with Bernardo directing and writing, it's bound to make some noise. Bernardo is a real heavyweight in the business.

MARTHA. How come I've never hear of him?

STEVE. It's one of those secrets of the business. Only those in the know, know.

MARTHA. Know what?

STEVE. Know that Bernardo can practically walk on water.

MARTHA. Those who can't do, teach.

STEVE. He likes teaching. Anyway, you'll like this. I get to play a young lawyer.

MARTHA. You would have made a terrific lawyer. Lawyers do a lot of acting, and you could have been a litigator.

STEVE. I'm actually getting ready to go out. Thanks for the supplies.

MARTHA. Is there anything else I can do for you?

Pause.

STEVE. Well, now that you mention it, can we discuss a little financial aid? It's not just the classes, it's the rent...and sometimes we actually eat.

MARTHA. Oy veh, has it come to this?

STEVE. Mom, you're not looking at it from the proper perspective. You've got to think of this as an extension of college. Grad school but without the degree.

MARTHA. All this money and no degree? Oy gevalt.

STEVE. It's like an artisan learning a craft. Like an apprentice.

MARTHA. Then you would at least have something to show for it. It's just this so-called "livelihood"—and I use the term very loosely—that you've chosen is so unpredictable.

STEVE. I know we've been through this a thousand times before. This is my chosen profession, and it takes time to establish yourself. For heaven's sake, Mel's folks don't give her half the grief you give me.

MARTHA. Maybe her parents don't care as much about their child as we do. Did you ever stop to think about that? Maybe you want a new set of parents?

Pause.

STEVE. No, the old set of parents will do just fine.

MARTHA. Melinda mentioned a full-time job at the radio station?

STEVE. I know.

MARTHA. Is that something you'd like to discuss?

STEVE. The station is all right, but it's not in my future. It's just a stopgap measure for me on my way to having an acting career.

MARTHA. Look, sweetheart, let me tell you something. If you think you're special, you're not. You're just like everyone else. You've got bills to pay, and someday, God willing, a wife and children to support. But the sea doesn't part for you. You always want me to be honest with you? Well, I'm being honest.

STEVE. Well, you know what I think? I think I am a unique individual. One of a kind and very, very special. I march to my own drummer. I will not settle for a middle management dead-end job.

MARTHA. Your father is not middle management. He owns that eraser company. He's not known as "The Eraser King" for nothing: *(singing)* "You Can Never Make a Mistake That Cannot Be Erased."

STEVE. My dream in life is not to buy the biggest house or drive the fanciest car…or be the heir to the "Eraser Kingdom." It's not what life is about for me.

MARTHA. You're talking like a child. This kind of talk is okay for a college student. This dreaming is fine for philosophy classes, but you're an adult now. I know you, I'm your mother. You like the finer things in life.

STEVE. Who doesn't? And, yes, dreams do come at a price. That's what we're paying for here. I'm paying with my life. You're paying…

MARTHA. …with cash.

STEVE. I appreciate your help—I really do. Look, I really have to get ready now. As the dates firm up, I'll let you and Dad know. Thanks again for everything.

MARTHA. How much do you need?

STEVE. Whatever you can spare.

> *He kisses her and exits to the bedroom. Martha writes out a check and leaves it on the table. She places her coffee and cookies in the kitchen. She exits. We see Steve dressing. He thinks Martha is still there.*

You know, Mom, I don't know if being at the station has a future or not. But it seems I spend my whole Goddamn life preparing for the future. Junior high, preparing for high school, preparing for college, for life: marriage, family, retirement and death. My whole life is lived for a future that never arrives. Oh, Christ, Mom. I feel like I spend my life waiting in the wings for my cue, which nobody gives me. I'm ready to cut loose. I'm ready to take center stage. But I never get a chance to go on. I want a chance to live my life the way I want to, and theater will be my life. I mean, hell, what's the surprise? I've been working toward this since I was a kid. When all my friends went to Woodstock, I went to summer stock. What can I say? Dreams do die hard.

> *He enters the room and sees he is alone. He sees the check.*

And I love you and Dad. And thanks for everything, Amen.

END OF ACT I SCENE III

ACT I SCENE IV

The opening night party is winding down. The revelers are in the hall and don't want to leave. There are a few coats lying around as well as beer bottles chips, etc.

NICKY. Great opening night! We're gonna go get a brewskie! Come on you two-skie…

BERNARDO. I'll be with you in a minute. Just give us five minutes alone.

> *Nicky leaves.*

Come in, my lamb, come into the lion's den.

MELINDA. Oh, Bernardo, what a wonderful show, what a wonderful night. Did I please you?

BERNARDO. Darling you were a gem, a flawless diamond: pure, clear, multifaceted.

MELINDA. You really think so?

BERNARDO. Not just me, my pet, the word is the papers loved you, and—dare I say it out loud?—the actor-writer-director moi! Do you hear me Papa?! You are vindicated! The producers are in hog heaven or producer's heaven, if there is at all a difference between the two.

MELINDA. Tell me.

BERNARDO. Well, my sweet, one said, I forget which, "a new face with the voice of an angel has graced the New York stage," or something like that. They talked about youth, freshness, innocence…But as for me, they proclaimed, "the master is back." Who am I to argue with the critics? Congratulations to us both.

> *He kisses her on both cheeks and full on the mouth.*

MELINDA. Oh.

BERNARDO. Mais, pas encore. There is more. The producers, delightful deep-pocketed lot that they are, have seen fit to move the show to Broadway.

MELINDA. Oh, my God. I mean, mon dieu…

BERNARDO. Now you're getting into the spirit of things. We move in December.

MELINDA. So soon?

BERNARDO. Time is money, ma petite. Now, as to Steven. As you know, my child, life isn't always fair. You've got to take the good with the bad, the wine with the vinegar…

MELINDA. The what?

BERNARDO. …the horosettes with the bitter herbs…

MELINDA. I don't…

BERNARDO. …to make an omelet you have to break a few eggs. We knew from the start he was a little young to play Cohn. But the acting pool being what it is and at the salaries we aren't paying, the choices were somewhat limited to say the least. With time being of the essence, casting him seemed to be the most expedient answer to a difficult situation. We took a chance and we failed. It's as simple as that. No recriminations, no looking back. Not that he was bad, my lamb, just not good enough…simply not what we're looking for.

MELINDA. What are you saying?

BERNARDO. They want to fire Steven.

MELINDA. Oh, no.

BERNARDO. It's not me, lamb, it's the producers. They want someone who plays older…shall we say, a more seasoned performer?

MELINDA. But Steven was good. He did everything you told him. He worked so hard. How were his notices?

BERNARDO. Not, as we say, my pet, money reviews. I fought them tooth and nail, lamb, I did.

MELINDA. He can get better. You know he would do anything.

BERNARDO. Steve's young, Melinda. Young in mind and spirit. When he's forty-five, if he can retain that quality, after life tries to beat it out of him, and it will, he'll be a dear, like me.

MELINDA. You're forty-five?

BERNARDO. Who told you that? But now we need an actor who has been knocked around a bit, rough around the edges.

There's a pounding at the door.

NICKY. Hey, Bernardo, let me in! I forgot my shades.

He lets Nicky in.

BERNARDO. Nicky was my recommendation to the producers…

MELINDA. Oh, my.

BERNARDO. …and they accepted it. Remember, it's all for the good of the show. This is no time for melancholy,

Melinda. My dears, as we say in show business…well, that's show business. Tonight we dance, my pet, and tomorrow we'll pay the piper. You two celebrate.

> *He plants a kiss on each cheek and another full-mouthed kiss on her.*

Remember, my pets, acting is all about honesty. If you can fake that, then you've got it made.

> *Bernardo exits.*

NICKY. Congratulations. I told you it would be me and you, kid.

MELINDA. You did, didn't you?

NICKY. Come on. Like the man said, it's all for the good of the show. And, what can I say? The better man won.

> *He gives her a big kiss and exits. After a moment we hear a toilet flush, and Steve enters from the bathroom. He has heard everything.*

STEVE. I guess congratulations are in order. Can I kiss you? Everyone else has.

MELINDA. Did you hear everything?

STEVE. I'm being replaced with Nicky.

MELINDA. Nobody could ever replace you, Steven. Besides, you are still an actor using his "instrument."

STEVE. Aw, come off it, Mel. You want to become an actor, then act. I didn't get into this profession to announce record labels. Shakespeare, Shaw, new and exciting works…

MELINDA. I believe in you. I believe in you, voice, body and soul.

STEVE. Will it change us?

MELINDA. I will be on time with my rent now.

STEVE. I'll dance at your Broadway debut.

MELINDA. We'll meet new people, important people, people-who-can-further-our-career kind of people.

STEVE. A new life, together?

MELINDA. Inseparable.

> *They embrace. His eyes are closed and hers are wide open.*

> *END OF ACT I SCENE IV*

ACT II SCENE I

It is two weeks before Christmas and the apartment is a mess. Boxes, cosmetics, and clothes are scattered over the room. Steven has set up a nice candlelit dinner for two. The telephone rings. Steven enters from the kitchen wearing an apron and beating some eggs in a bowl. He answers the phone in a Swedish dialect.

STEVE. Ya? Ya, dis iz da Donahoo hoose. Yumpin' yimminey, I don't know ven she get back. Can I take a message? Uh-huh. Who? David Merrick? Big Broadway producer? Oh, big big Broadway producer. Yass, soon as she gets in. Me? Ya, I'm da new cook. Gooden byen.

> *He hangs up.*

Wow! David Merrick!

> *He enters the kitchen on one side and reenters from the other side when the phone rings again. He answers like Elmer Fudd.*

Hewo? Who is this pwease? Heh-heh-heh-heh-heh. Oh, Way Cowins the new pubwacist? Oh. Okay, how do you spell that? Cwive Bauns? Cwive Bauns, the cwitic? Okey, dokey. Now he is a waskley wabbit. Okey, dokey.

> *Hangs up. The phone rings again. He answers in an oriental dialect.*

Harro? No. Missy not at home. Marinda never alound…never ever! Mom! Oh, hi. What's up? No, I'm fine—just learning how to cope. Sorry you won't be able to make the opening, but when Florida calls, one must answer. How was Cousin Bernie's bar mitzvah? Wow! He got how much?

> *Melinda enters carrying an assortment of boxes and packages. She puts the packages on the sofa and coffee table and takes out a wig on a styrofoam head.*

STEVE. Oops. Gotta go, Mom, the baby's crying. I'll speak to you later.

> *Hangs up.*

Hi, sweetie.

MELINDA. What do you think of this wig? I think it's divine. I saw it at Saks and I put it on. The sales girl said I looked liked like Olivia Newton-John. Who could resist?

STEVE. Well, I think…

MELINDA. Oh, God, we got cocktails with that columnist from the *Post*.

STEVE. You meeting Leonard Lyons?

MELINDA. Last week.

STEVE. Earl Wilson?

MELINDA. Yesterday.

STEVE. Joey Adams?

MELINDA. Yes. Oh, Steve, I miss you too.

STEVE. I was hoping to have a quiet dinner for two. A chance to get acquainted again.

MELINDA. Christ, I bought this outfit this morning. I hope it's the right thing. Oh, and this wig will save me a lot of energy. Instead of washing and drying all the time. Have there been any messages? Did the phone ring?

STEVE. Like the *Jerry Lewis Telethon*. And Steve Leonards called twenty times, the old bore. Wants to have dinner with you. Won't take no for an answer.

The phone rings.

MELINDA. Oh, Stevie, of course. You've been just wonderful.

Melinda picks up.

Hi, Melinda Donahugh here. Oh, Nicky, hi lamb, what's up? Now? I was actually planning to…

STEVE. I was wondering if we could have dinner alone some night?

MELINDA. Another photo call. They'll have to pay overtime.

STEVE *(imitating Groucho Marx).* Sounds good to me, but who wants to have a lonesome night? How's about a ride on the Staten Island Ferry?

MELINDA. That sounds exciting.

STEVE. Oh, you like that? How about dancing at Roseland?

MELINDA. I'd love to.

STEVE *(as Groucho).* How's your rumba?

STEVE *(continued)*. I don't know, how's Uganda? How's Uranus? Let's not go there. Hail Freedonia…

MELINDA *(to Steve)*. Hold on a minute, would you?

> *She covers the phone.*

Will you shut the fuck up when I'm on the phone?

> *They stare at each other. Steve sings.*

STEVE. She talks, like an angel talks/She walks, like an angel walks.

> *Melinda starts to be charmed.*

MELINDA. I'll have to call you back.

> *She hangs up.*

STEVE. And her hair has a kind of curl/To my mind, she's my kind of girl.

MELINDA. This is serious.

STEVE. She cooks, like an angel cooks/

MELINDA. You know I can't cook.

STEVE. She looks, like an angel looks/

MELINDA *(laughing)*. You're incorrigible, do you know that?

STEVE. And her smile puts me in a whirl/To my mind she's my kind of girl.

(He starts to kiss her.)

MELINDA. No, no, no. I have important things do and I haven't got time to play.

She grabs the wig and goes into the bedroom.

STEVE. I'll save the candles. My wick will have to wait. How about a midnight supper of you and me?

MELINDA. Do you know what happened to my other boot?

STEVE. What am I? A fortune-teller? I don't know where your boot ran off to. Come on, how about it?

Limping in with one boot on.

MELINDA. There it is. Would you hand it to me?

STEVE *(grabbing it first)*. What's it worth to you?

Melinda grabs it.

MELINDA. Sorry sweetkins, but I haven't got time for this. How do I look?

STEVE. Like a star.

MELINDA. You're a dear. See you later. Don't wait up.

Melinda exits.

STEVE *(talking the head, imitating Humphrey Bogart).* Well sweetheart, I have the feeling this is beginning of a beautiful friendship.

We hear "As Time Goes By."

END OF ACT II SCENE I

ACT II SCENE II

Voice-over:

Alright Nicky, listen to me. Steve's Roy Cohn was too cute, too nice, too intelligent. We want someone who can play more of a dim bulb, a moron, an idiot. Someone like you. Let's see if we can make this work. Act 5, Scene 4! Imagine you're a man who for his entire life has kept everything bottled up inside. Political secrets and personal secrets alike are clogging his system—physically as well as metaphorically. All this shit has backed up in him. His bladder is bursting. He has been constipated his whole life and it's time to let it go. Be open and cleanse your system as well as you soul. Let it go! Let it all go! Whenever you're ready.

Spotlight on Nicky. He freezes.

NICKY. I gotta go to the bathroom. I gotta go to the bathroom.

BERNARDO. Take five, everybody.

Blackout.

Vlad, get the mop, will you?

END OF ACT II SCENE II

ACT II SCENE III

It is three days before Christmas. There are a small tree and a menorah side by side on the table. Melinda and Bernardo are rehearsing a scene from I Married a Communist. *She walks over to the chair.*

MELINDA. You've been through an enormous pseudo-Slavic day in court, you poor, poor, crazy czar of my heart. When you face the committee tomorrow, I know you will do the perspicacious thing. Tomorrow, the world will comprehend the meaning of the word "hero." If there is anything I can give you, or maybe do for you, I have such an overpowering urge to make a personal sacrifice for the revolution.

> *We hear Steve singing in the hallway. He enters.*

STEVE. We wish you a Merry Christmas…

> *He notices Melinda and Bernardo.*

Oh, I'm sorry—were you guys rehearsing?

MELINDA. We thought we'd do some line run-throughs. Keep it sharp, you know.

BERNARDO. Yes, my lambs, you cannot rehearse too much.

STEVE. You can never get enough, huh, Bernardo?

BERNARDO. You get one shot at the prize, one chance to grasp the brass ring…Carpe diem, my boy. Seize the moment.

STEVE. So how's the show going?

BERNARDO. Well, our actress here is très merveilleux. There seems to be no limit to what she can do.

MELINDA. I'll see you at…I'll see you, Bernardo.

BERNARDO. But of course. Comrades, the revolution is at hand! My only regret is that I can't sit in the audience and watch me.

Bernardo exits.

MELINDA. What are you doing home so early?

STEVE. Early from what? I went out. I came back.

MELINDA. I just thought you had an extra shift at the station.

STEVE. I'm happy to see you home alone for a change. I never see you anymore.

MELINDA. Here I am.

STEVE. The mind understands and laughs—ha, ha, ha—but the heart, she-a break inna thousand pieces.

MELINDA. You're just upset. Don't worry.

STEVE. Are you having an affair?

MELINDA. Let's get something straight. I like you. I think you are a sweet, kind…

STEVE. "Like" me.

MELINDA. Yes, I like you enormously. And I could never have gotten here without you. However, now I do have a career to think about. I can't spend half of my time here fucking around…

STEVE. Literally or figuratively?

MELINDA. Both! Neither! Oh, Steve, can't you just cool it, please?

STEVE. Any cooler and we'll be in cryogenic suspension.

MELINDA. Everything's a joke to you, isn't it? Would you just stop fooling around?

STEVE. Look who's talking about fooling around. Who's fooling who? Who's the bigger fool?

MELINDA. I think it's time we discussed my moving into my own apartment.

STEVE. What?

MELINDA. You're such a romantic. I think you like living like this. Sometimes I think you even thrive on it. But people change, and I don't want to live like this forever.

STEVE. This is called "paying your dues."

MELINDA. You're so naïve I'm almost envious.

STEVE. Hold on a second, baby. I've invested almost two years of my life in this relationship…

MELINDA. You're talking two years ago—ancient history. I'm talking about now. I'm not getting any younger either.

STEVE. You're twenty-five years old.

  Pause.

MELINDA. I'm twenty-nine.

STEVE. But you told me…

MELINDA. Never mind what I told you.

STEVE. You're breaking up with me?

MELINDA. I'm moving out.

STEVE. You can't move out.

MELINDA. Why not?

STEVE. Because I don't want you to. Because you and I finally found each other and lived together for two years because we wanted to. Not because we had to. Give us some time together to work this out.

MELINDA. Time! This is my time. Mine. There are so many producers, press agents, directors, dinners, luncheons, and parties going on. And they invite me, Steven, not us. They want me. And Steve, that's just the trimmings. The Christmas Dinner is finally getting recognition for my work, my talent. Suddenly, all those years of self-doubt, those constant rejections at auditions, the heartbreak in my parents' eyes when they couldn't do any more to help me. Suddenly, it means something. Yes, I mean something. I make a difference. Steven, it really is Christmas. How else can I make you understand?

STEVE. I understand we were helping each other.

MELINDA. Right now, I don't need your help. All I need is one outfit and my bathroom stuff.

STEVE. Where are you going to go? Where are you going to stay?

MELINDA. Here's the phone number where I can be reached. If anyone is looking for me, they can reach me there.

> *She writes down a number, hands it to him and exits.*

STEVE. This is Bernardo's number.

> *END OF ACT II SCENE III*

ACT II SCENE IV

Later that evening: The apartment is in shambles. A large bottle of vodka is half empty and an empty carton of orange juice lies on its side. There's a half-finished screwdriver on the table. We can hear Steven singing.

> *The phone rings.*

STEVE. Loves Labor's Lost here. Pete, man, how you doin'? Not so good. Mel left me and…what? What do you mean I'm supposed to be at the station? Now? Tonight? What time is it? Oh my god. Oh Pete, look, I'm in no shape to broadcast tonight. Patch me in? On the phone? You can do that? What do you mean sixty seconds? Pete, you can't do this to me. I mean it, man. You want me to wing it? I'm not a DJ, I'm an actor.

> *He thinks about his last remark.*

Okay, Pete, count me in—I said count…three, two, one.

> *He's on the air.*

Happy holidays to all my listeners out there. This is Steve Leonards saying I hope that your holidays are going better than mine. Tonight, I'm going to stray from the usual classical format, perhaps get a little philosophical, and talk about what the holidays really mean to me. Peace on earth, good will toward men. Men! This is the true meaning of the holidays. It's really a celebration of men! Sure, women try to whitewash it. They invented Mrs. Claus for that very reason. There was St. Nick, but no Mrs. St. Nick. At Chanukah, who do we celebrate? Judah Maccabee and his brothers! The Maccabees! They don't talk about Mrs. Maccabee. Mrs. Maccabee sounds Irish, doesn't it? Well, there are Irish Jews, I suppose. But most of all, let's talk about the "big guy." "He's" got the whole world in his hands. "He" took a hundred pounds of clay. "He" created the world in seven days and "He" created man. Together, they created woman. At no small cost to man's health, I might add. Removing a rib, by any stretch of the imagination, is no minor operation. But Adam had it good. He didn't have to listen to Eve talk about all the other guys she dated before him or worry about any other competition. I miss the old days. Let me cut right to the chase. My girlfriend just dumped me. After giving her two of the best years of my life. I know, I know, I can't believe it either, but there you go. That's like ten percent of my life…up in smoke…pffffft. This is a lonely time of year for men anyway. But to be unceremoniously cast aside at this moment in time, at this joyous, ha, time of the year, is heresy, maybe even sacrilegious.

He starts creating a row of wet toilet paper balls and throwing them at Melinda's picture.

So I am appealing to all you men out there to arise and unite as one. For this one time let history know where you stand: straight or gay, black or white, rich or poor, young or old. Anyone with the courage and conviction to say "I matter." So here's what I want you to do.

He reads off the paper Melinda gave him.

I want you to call 863-2975. That's a 212 area code, and whoever answers, I want you to ask to speak to Melinda Donahugh. And when she gets on the phone I want you to say "Season's Greetings, you Christmas bitch and holiday ball buster!" Yes, you heard me. "Christmas bitch and holiday ball buster!" And tell her it's from you and Steve Leonards. If the line is busy, good, try again. It means our message is getting through because of people like you. I say, "To hell—can I say that on radio? Well, what the hell? I say to hell with Women's Lib." It's Men's Liberation I'm talking about. I've been told it is time for toughening up, and by heavens it is. Some holiday seasoning, if you will. So, to all you men out there, tonight we strike a blow for you, me and all mankind. Say what you will, it is truly the shallow who really know themselves. If the station hasn't thrown me off the air and if they don't censor me, I will be back here at six o'clock Christmas Eve. Join me and others like you to celebrate the joy, the wonder, the vitality that is Man!

> *Blackout. A phone starts to ring. It is soon joined by hundreds of other phones ringing. It rises to a deafening pitch, then stops.*

> *END OF ACT II SCENE IV*

ACT II SCENE V

A few days later: There are some slight changes to the room: an erotic piece of African art—a naked man— stands on the coffee table and a throw is covering the sofa. As the curtain rises, we see the door to the bedroom close and hear the shower being turned on. After a moment, Melinda enters from the front door, carrying her suitcase. She hears the water running and sighs. She goes to the door and shouts.

MELINDA. Steve? It's me Melinda. I just came by to pick up a few things. I didn't know you were going to be here. Frankly, I was hoping you'd be at the station.

The shower stops.

Let's not play that same old scene again. I want you to know that I still have deep affection for you, Steve. I feel this way even after some of the things I heard you said about me on the air—that were heard by over two million people, I might add. The years that we spent together were terrific. You are…were great in the sack, really. It's just…this is tough to say talking to a door. You were a great support for me when I was down. Really, you are…were…no, are still important to me. Look, why don't I wait until you come out so we can talk?

The bedroom door opens and Martha comes out in a bathrobe, drying her hair. They see each other.

What are you doing here?

MARTHA. What are you doing here?

MELINDA. I thought you were Steve.

MARTHA. Remind me to sue my plastic surgeon.

MELINDA. I came to collect some things.

MARTHA *(looking at the suitcase)*. Thank heavens—I thought you were moving back in.

MELINDA. I figured Steve would be at the station. I thought it would be better if he wasn't here.

MARTHA. You already stole his heart from him—isn't that enough?

Pause.

I didn't know you still had a key.

MELINDA. I guess he didn't want to change the locks.

MARTHA. Well, you can't think of everything. I'll make it a priority.

Writing on a pad on the table.

"Things to do": change the locks… and buy some bagels.

MELINDA. What are you doing here?

MARTHA. Not that I owe you any explanations, but Steven is moving out to a new apartment—Riverside Drive, I believe. He had three months left on his lease here, so his father and I decided to use it as a pied-à-terre. The Salvation Army is coming tomorrow to clean out some of this "stuff." I suppose some of your treasured heirlooms might be among the "soon-to-be-departing"? You did some interesting decorating. Eclectic schlock?

MELINDA. Isn't this a rough neighborhood for you? A little bit too Bohemian, perhaps?

MARTHA. Honey, I was born on the Lower East Side. It's changed a bit, but you'd be surprised how much is the same.

MELINDA. I can't believe this.

MARTHA. Can't believe what?

MELINDA. That after all these years of nagging and
pestering Steve for living down here, you're moving in
yourself.

MARTHA. With a little imagination, a good decorator,
and this den could be quite livable.

MELINDA. Civilization is not defined by Bloomingdale's.

MARTHA. But it is, dear, it is.

MELINDA *(picking up the naked man)*. What style would
you call this? "Oedipus Primitive"?

MARTHA. Touché. I'm telling you I've discovered some
wonderful art galleries in the area. People change.
I believe that's what you said to my son? Sy and I
haven't done this kind of thing in years. Look, why
don't you just leave the key and call it a day.

Melinda slams the key down.

MELINDA. You know, I think Steve is a fine boy.

MARTHA. Great in the sack, so you said. Just what every
mother wants to hear. But you broke his heart.

MELINDA. I didn't mean to. I'm under a lot of pressure
too. Unlike Steven, my parents can't afford to support
me.

MARTHA. Don't talk to me about being poor, young lady. My father was a poor tailor who put me through college and my three brothers through medical school. And yes, we lived on the sixth floor and never complained. Don't talk to me about being poor.

MELINDA. The show I'm in…that Steve was in…is going great guns…and my star is rising.

MARTHA. Oh, I see, Miss Rising Star. I see that you throw people away at the slightest provocation. I don't meddle in my son's affairs, but it's only one silly role.

MELINDA. It's not one role. It's "the" role. The role of a lifetime.

MARTHA. There'll be plenty of roles, believe you me. But you'll never come across a "Steve Leonards" again.

MELINDA. I know that, but opportunity doesn't knock often. So, when it does, you better be ready to answer it with a big smile and open arms.

MARTHA. Like I said, I don't meddle in my son's affairs, but let me just say this one thing. He's looking for stability in this facactah industry you call "show business." Personally, I don't think it can exist in such a world. If you're not the one to give that to him, then it's best you leave.

MELINDA. Did you hear his Christmas broadcast? Did you hear the things he said about me?

MARTHA. Why, was any of it true?

MELINDA. Let's just say he exaggerated the truth to get a laugh at my expense. He turned my life upside down. It drove my publicist crazy.

MARTHA. So get a new publicist, not a new boyfriend. But, if that's the way you feel, you're right to be rid of him. People do change. Look at my son. Who would have thought? A macha on the radio. He really is special. I didn't think radio was that big, but what do I know?

Pause.

MELINDA. Look, I haven't got time for this. I'm a very busy woman. I have appointments I'm already late for.

She starts to exit, but stops by the menorah sitting on the shelf.

I bought him that menorah for Chanukah last year. You know, I'm not Jewish.

MARTHA *(she sighs).* I know. Nobody's perfect.

Pause.

MARTHA. How about maybe you keep the key a little while longer? In case you want to avoid Steven, he'll be here next Thursday morning around elevenish.

Melinda takes the key and exits.

END OF ACT II SCENE V

ACT II SCENE VI

One week later. Steve is packing up and getting ready to move out. He goes into the bedroom with some tape. Melinda enters wearing a fur coat.

MELINDA. Hello? Hello?

> *Steve enters with a box.*

STEVE *(thinking it's the movers)*. I didn't hear you ring up. Just grab that box out there…oh, it's you. What do you want?

MELINDA. Is it safe?

STEVE. Safe?

MELINDA. You know, for the holiday ball buster to come in.

STEVE. I calls 'em like I sees 'em. You got off easy. I thought of a lot nastier stuff later on.

MELINDA. The phone rang for three days, so we took it off the hook. Bernardo was furious.

STEVE. If he can't take a joke, fuck 'im. Oh, I forgot—you already did that, didn't you?

Pause. he goes back to packing.

MELINDA. I hear you're doing much better as a single act than we did as a double.

STEVE. Is that so?

MELINDA. It's all over the columns. You've created a whole new style of tell-it-like-it-is radio.

STEVE. As a matter of fact, they're giving me my own show. They're changing the classical format to all talking and they want me to anchor it. They got more mail and phone calls from my Christmas show than any other broadcast in the history of the station.

MELINDA. That was a wild show. You were pretty rough on me.

STEVE. You listened?

MELINDA. No, but everyone I know did. It was three weeks until they stopped referring to me by that charming moniker you gave me.

STEVE. I'd say don't take it too personally, but I want you to. Yes, every year it'll be Santa, Rudolph, and you. "The Christmas…"

MELINDA. I get the point.

STEVE. Here's the rest of your stuff. That's a nice-looking coat.

MELINDA. You like it? I bought it on credit. Fake fur… feel it.

STEVE. Nice.

MELINDA. Anyway, take a good look. It goes back in two days.

STEVE. How come?

MELINDA. You didn't hear?

STEVE. Frankly, I've been too busy to follow your career.

MELINDA. For real, you don't know? This auto-biographical play, *I Married a Communist,* was a hoax. They found out the whole thing was a fraud. Bernardo lied about everything. No Hollywood Eleven, no standing before the committee.

STEVE. No blacklisting.

MELINDA. His father was a dentist from Ohio. He's about as Russian as Russian dressing.

STEVE. All fake! Wow. Talk about your Stanislavski.

MELINDA. But wait—there's more. Think of this as part of my confession, okay? Forgive me, Father Leonards, for I have sinned.

STEVE. Rabbi Leonards, to you. So, what happened?

MELINDA. When you got the role of Roy Cohn, initially, Nicky was furious. So he contacted his old friends at Pinkerton. They're the ones who found out Bernardo lied about everything. Nicky used it to blackmail Bernardo into giving him your role.

STEVE. You mean I lost the role to that idiot because he threatened Bernardo?

MELINDA. Yes. Then the press got wind of it and it started to snowball. Now the show's a bigger hit than ever!

STEVE. So he blackmailed Bernardo and now the show's a smash? Instead of *I Married A Communist* they shoulda called it *The American Way*.

    Pause.

I knew it. I knew it. I knew it wasn't because of my acting. I was good, wasn't I?

MELINDA. Yes, Steven, you were very good.

STEVE. So, what's the deal with you and Bernardo now?

MELINDA. He skipped town. He bought an ashram in San Francisco. Who but a great conman could try and pull off a hoax like this?

STEVE. So, what now?

MELINDA. I told you, return the coat.

STEVE. That's not what I meant.

MELINDA. I'm going to go out to L.A. My brother is finally directing a movie and he thinks he can use me. I just came over to say good-bye.

STEVE. That was a rough deal you handed me.

MELINDA. You got me pretty good.

STEVE. Seeing you again isn't my idea of a good time.

MELINDA. You know us Catholics, we love to confess.

STEVE. There's nothing to talk about.

MELINDA. You're not going to make this easy for me, are you?

STEVE. You didn't make it easy for me.

MELINDA. I got caught up in the storm. It was a whirlwind. Can you believe I fell for it? The "big time acting teacher" pays attention to the groundling. I'm asking for your forgiveness, Rabbi Leonards.

STEVE. You tore my guts out.

MELINDA. You could have been more patient.

STEVE. All I wanted was to be with you.

MELINDA. You're selfish.

STEVE. You're self-centered.

MELINDA. You're spoiled.

STEVE. You're heartless.

Melinda grabs the menorah off the shelf.

MELINDA. You're not taking this with you.

He starts to chase her around the sofa.

STEVE. That was a present.

MELINDA. Yeah, from me.

They race around the big chair.

STEVE. That's a religious artifact!

> *Steve cuts her off. They are staring at each other panting for breath. They kiss.*

I love you, Mel. I always did.

MELINDA. Oh Steve, I'm so sorry. But they say the making up part is the best part.

STEVE. Yes indeed.

> *(The phone rings.)*

Hello, Steve "shock-jock" Leonards here.

> *(To Melinda.)*

I made that up myself. Catchy, don't you think?

> *(Listens. To Melinda.)*

It's my agent.

> *(In the phone.)*

Not another *Times* interview. Lunch with David Suskind and Scott Muni? Not together, I hope. Well, my time is extremely valuable, so how soon can I see a contract?

MELINDA *(Singing).* He looks…like an angel looks.

STEVE *(in the phone).* Hold on a minute.

MELINDA *(continuing the song).* He schtups, like a lover schtups.

STEVE *(to Melinda).* Where'd you learn that word? *(In the phone.)* I'll call you back.

MELINDA. When he smiles, stars shine in the sky/To my mind, he's my kind of guy.

STEVE *(hanging up the phone).* What am I going to do with you?

MELINDA. Everything.

> *CURTAIN*